BEVERLY WARNE

BIPOLAR DISORDER
SURVIVAL COOKBOOK

BONUS 28 DAYS MEAL PLAN

Table of content

Introduction

Empowering Your Journey Through Food and Resilience

Living with bipolar disorder can feel like navigating a stormy sea—where mood swings, unpredictable challenges, and deep emotional shifts often disrupt the calm. In the midst of these turbulent waters, finding stability might seem elusive. Yet, nourishment—both of the body and the spirit—holds the transformative power to bring balance, comfort, and hope.

This cookbook is more than just a collection of recipes; it's a survival guide and a celebration of resilience. It is built on the understanding that what you eat can directly influence how you feel. Here, you will find thoughtfully curated meals designed to support mental clarity, stabilize mood, and provide the energy needed to face each day with renewed strength. Each recipe has been crafted with care, keeping in mind the delicate interplay between nutrition and mental well-being.

In these pages, you are invited to embark on a journey where food becomes a tool for healing. As you prepare these dishes, you are not only feeding your body but also nurturing your mind—creating a foundation of stability during both the highs and lows of your experience. This cookbook is a testament to the power of small, intentional changes that add up to a more balanced, vibrant life.

May this book inspire you to reclaim control, embrace nourishment, and find solace in the art of cooking. Let each recipe be a stepping stone towards a more resilient, empowered version of yourself.

Understanding Bipolar Disorder and Nutrition

Bipolar disorder is a complex mental health condition characterized by significant mood swings ranging from depressive lows to manic highs. While traditional treatments include medication and therapy, emerging evidence suggests that lifestyle factors—especially nutrition—play a critical role in managing symptoms and supporting brain health. Food is not merely fuel; it's a dynamic tool that influences brain chemistry, inflammation, and the balance of hormones, all of which can impact mood stability. In this chapter, we explore the intersection between bipolar disorder and nutrition, highlighting how targeted dietary choices can contribute to stability and wellness.

Eating for Stability and Wellness

A consistent, balanced diet lays the foundation for physical and mental well-being, which is particularly important for individuals managing bipolar disorder. Eating for stability and wellness involves more than counting calories—it means choosing foods that support a steady energy supply, enhance brain function, and reduce inflammation.

For many living with bipolar disorder, erratic eating patterns can mirror or even trigger mood fluctuations. Skipping meals, overindulging, or consuming foods high in sugar and unhealthy fats may lead to rapid shifts in blood sugar levels and energy, potentially exacerbating mood instability. Instead, a diet rich in whole foods, lean proteins, and healthy fats can help maintain a balanced mood. Establishing regular meal times and portion control can provide structure, reducing the likelihood of impulsive eating that might trigger symptoms.

Moreover, incorporating a diverse range of nutrient-dense foods ensures that the brain receives a steady supply of vitamins, minerals, and antioxidants crucial for neurotransmitter production and overall brain health. A mindful approach to eating—where the focus is on quality, timing, and balance—can offer a sense of control and empowerment, which is essential for navigating the ups and downs of bipolar disorder.

The Bipolar Brain and Diet: How Food Affects Mood

The human brain is an intricate network of neurons and chemical messengers that orchestrate every emotion, thought, and behavior. In individuals with bipolar disorder, this delicate balance can be disrupted, leading to extreme mood swings. However, food plays a vital role in modulating these processes by influencing neurotransmitter production, inflammation levels, and even the gut microbiome—a community of microorganisms that communicate directly with the brain through what's known as the gut-brain axis.

Certain nutrients are essential for the synthesis of neurotransmitters like serotonin, dopamine, and gamma-aminobutyric acid (GABA), all of which are implicated in mood regulation. For example, amino acids such as tryptophan and tyrosine—found in lean meats, dairy, and legumes—are precursors to serotonin and dopamine, respectively. When these building blocks are plentiful, the brain can more effectively produce the chemical messengers that help stabilize mood.

Beyond neurotransmitter synthesis, diet also affects inflammation, a factor that increasingly is recognized in mental health research. Diets high in processed foods, refined sugars, and unhealthy fats tend to promote systemic inflammation, which may worsen mood symptoms. In contrast, an anti-inflammatory diet—rich in fruits, vegetables, whole grains, and omega-3 fatty acids—can reduce inflammation and support brain health.

Furthermore, the gut microbiome is gaining recognition as a key player in mental health. The foods you eat can shape the composition of gut bacteria, which in turn produce neuroactive compounds that influence mood. A diet high in fiber and fermented foods, such as yogurt or kefir, helps cultivate a healthy microbiome, potentially aiding in the stabilization of mood swings.

Understanding how food interacts with brain chemistry provides valuable insights into why specific dietary choices can be so beneficial—or detrimental—for those living with bipolar disorder.

Essential Nutrients for Mood Regulation

Certain nutrients are particularly critical for individuals with bipolar disorder, as they support brain function and help regulate mood. Integrating these nutrients into your daily diet can create a supportive environment for emotional balance.

Omega-3 Fatty Acids:

Omega-3s, found in fatty fish like salmon, mackerel, and sardines, as well as in flaxseeds and walnuts, are renowned for their anti-inflammatory properties and their ability to enhance neuronal function. Studies suggest that omega-3 fatty acids can help reduce the frequency and intensity of mood swings by modulating brain cell membranes and neurotransmitter function.

B Vitamins:

The B-vitamin family—especially B6, B12, and folate—is essential for energy production and the synthesis of neurotransmitters. These vitamins help convert food into energy and are critical for the production of serotonin and dopamine. Leafy greens, legumes, fortified cereals, and lean proteins are excellent sources of these vital nutrients.

Magnesium:

Magnesium is involved in hundreds of biochemical reactions in the body, including those that regulate nerve function and mood. Deficiencies in magnesium have been linked to increased anxiety and depression. Incorporating magnesium-rich foods such as nuts, seeds, whole grains, and dark leafy greens can support a more stable mood.

Vitamin D:

Vitamin D receptors are abundant in the brain, and emerging research indicates that adequate levels of vitamin D may be crucial for mood regulation. Sunlight exposure is the primary source, but dietary sources like fortified dairy products, eggs, and fatty fish also contribute.

Antioxidants:

Oxidative stress can negatively impact brain function, so consuming a diet high in antioxidants is essential. Berries, dark chocolate, nuts, and a variety of fruits and vegetables help combat oxidative stress, supporting overall brain health and emotional well-being.

Amino Acids:

As the building blocks of neurotransmitters, amino acids like tryptophan and tyrosine are vital for mood regulation. Including lean protein sources such as chicken, turkey, tofu, and legumes can help ensure an adequate supply of these essential compounds.

By focusing on these nutrients, you can create a diet that not only fuels your body but also supports the biochemical processes underlying mood stability. Consistent intake of these foods may help mitigate some of the challenges associated with bipolar disorder.

Practical Strategies for Success

Living with bipolar disorder presents unique challenges that require a holistic approach to wellness. While medication and therapy remain central to treatment, lifestyle factors—especially nutrition—can significantly impact mood regulation. Practical strategies for success involve creating routines that stabilize energy levels and emotions while promoting overall health.

Establishing a Daily Routine:

One of the cornerstones of managing bipolar disorder is structure. A consistent daily routine helps regulate circadian rhythms, which in turn stabilizes mood. This includes set times for waking up, meals, exercise, and sleep. When your day follows a predictable pattern, your body and mind can better anticipate changes, reducing the likelihood of sudden mood swings.

Prioritizing Self-Care:

Self-care is multifaceted—it encompasses adequate sleep, regular physical activity, mindfulness practices, and, importantly, a balanced diet. Integrating self-care practices into your daily routine ensures that you are nurturing your body and mind. Activities such as yoga, meditation, or even a simple walk outdoors can contribute to emotional stability, especially when combined with mindful eating practices.

Tracking Your Progress:

Keeping a daily journal or mood diary can help identify patterns and triggers. Documenting what you eat, how you feel, and any symptoms you experience can provide insights over time. This self-monitoring not only supports better meal planning and routine adjustments but also serves as a conversation starter with your healthcare provider when fine-tuning your treatment plan.

Creating a Support System:

Managing bipolar disorder is not a journey meant to be taken alone. Engage with support networks, whether through family, friends, or bipolar-specific support groups. Connecting with others who share similar challenges and exchanging strategies can be a powerful and uplifting experience. A strong support system can also help reinforce the dietary and lifestyle changes that you are working hard to implement.

Mindful Eating Practices:

Mindful eating involves paying close attention to the taste, texture, and nutritional value of your food. This practice encourages you to slow down and savor each bite, reducing the risk of impulsive eating decisions that can lead to blood sugar spikes and mood fluctuations. By being present during meals, you can better gauge hunger and fullness cues, contributing to more balanced energy levels throughout the day.

Meal Prep Tips for Managing Mood Swings

Meal preparation is a powerful tool for managing the unpredictability of bipolar disorder. When mood swings disrupt your daily life, having pre-prepared, nutritious meals can ensure that you continue to receive balanced nutrition—even on challenging days.

Plan Ahead and Batch Cook:

When you're feeling well, take time to plan your meals for the week. Batch cooking meals like soups, stews, or casseroles allows you to store healthy options in the fridge or freezer. These ready-made meals can be a lifesaver on days when you lack the energy or motivation to cook. Batch cooking not only saves time but also ensures that you have control over the ingredients, avoiding processed foods that might trigger mood swings.

Create a Flexible Meal Plan:

Your meal plan should be structured yet adaptable. Some days, mood or energy levels may not allow you to stick strictly to a plan. Having a few quick, nutritious recipes that require minimal preparation can help. Simple meals like salads with lean proteins, whole-grain wraps, or overnight oats can be both satisfying and nutritionally balanced.

Invest in Proper Tools:

Quality kitchen tools can make meal preparation more enjoyable and less time-consuming. Consider investing in items like a slow cooker, pressure cooker, or food processor. These tools can help you create healthy meals with minimal active cooking time, reducing the stress associated with meal preparation during low-energy periods.

Portion Control and Balanced Snacks:

Planning doesn't stop at the main meals. Prepare healthy snacks such as cut vegetables, fruit portions, or homemade trail mix to maintain steady energy levels between meals. Pre-portioned snacks prevent overeating and help maintain a balance in blood sugar levels—an essential factor in mood regulation.

Mindful Preparation Environment:

Create an environment that makes meal prep an enjoyable ritual rather than a chore. Play soothing music, listen to a podcast, or invite a friend to cook with you. Making the process enjoyable increases the likelihood that you'll stick with your meal planning routine, reinforcing positive habits over time.

Weekly Review and Adjustments:

 Set aside time each week to review your meal plan. Reflect on what worked, what didn't, and what adjustments you might need to make. This ongoing process of evaluation and adaptation is critical, as it allows you to fine-tune your diet to better suit your evolving mood and energy levels.

How to Eat for Different Mood States: Depressive vs. Manic Episodes

Bipolar disorder is marked by contrasting mood states, each of which can affect appetite, energy levels, and nutritional needs. Tailoring your eating habits to these distinct phases can be a key strategy in managing symptoms effectively.

Eating During Depressive Episodes

When experiencing depressive episodes, it is common to feel a loss of appetite or a lack of motivation to prepare healthy meals. However, during these times, your body still requires nourishment to support recovery and energy.

Focus on Comforting, Nutrient-Dense Foods:
During depression, opt for foods that are both soothing and rich in essential nutrients. Warm, hearty soups, stews, and casseroles can provide comfort while ensuring you receive a balance of proteins, carbohydrates, and healthy fats. Including nutrient-dense foods such as leafy greens, lean proteins, and whole grains can help counteract the sluggishness associated with depression.

Small, Frequent Meals:
Large meals can seem overwhelming when energy is low. Instead, try eating smaller, more frequent meals or snacks throughout the day. This approach can help maintain blood sugar levels without requiring the energy to prepare and consume a full meal at once.

Include Omega-3 Fatty Acids:

Research suggests that omega-3 fatty acids may have mood-stabilizing effects. Incorporate sources such as salmon, mackerel, walnuts, and flaxseeds into your diet. These fats can support brain health and reduce inflammation, which is beneficial during depressive phases.

Stay Hydrated:

Dehydration can worsen feelings of fatigue and depression. Make a conscious effort to drink water throughout the day. Herbal teas and diluted fruit juices can also be beneficial, offering hydration along with antioxidants and vitamins.

Simple, Ready-to-Eat Options:

When motivation is low, having ready-to-eat, healthy options on hand can make a significant difference. Consider keeping items like Greek yogurt, nuts, fresh fruit, or whole-grain crackers accessible. These foods require little to no preparation and can provide quick bursts of energy and nutrition.

Eating During Manic Episodes

Manic episodes often come with heightened energy, rapid thoughts, and, at times, impulsivity in eating habits. During these periods, it's important to channel that energy into making choices that stabilize rather than exacerbate mood swings.

Balanced, Steady Meals:

Even though you might feel like eating constantly or indulging in impulsive choices, focus on meals that offer a steady release of energy. Complex carbohydrates, lean proteins, and healthy fats help prevent the rapid spikes and crashes associated with high-sugar or highly processed foods.

Limit Stimulants:

Manic phases can be marked by restlessness and an overactive mind. Limiting caffeine and other stimulants can help prevent these symptoms from worsening. Opt for herbal teas or decaffeinated alternatives to keep your energy levels balanced.

Mindful Portion Control:

Impulsive eating is a common challenge during mania. It can be helpful to pre-portion snacks and meals during periods of stability so that during manic episodes, you have controlled, balanced portions readily available. This practice can mitigate the risk of overeating or consuming excessive amounts of unhealthy foods.

Incorporate High-Fiber Foods:

Fiber helps regulate digestion and provides a sustained source of energy. Foods such as whole grains, legumes, fruits, and vegetables can stabilize blood sugar levels and help temper the rapid energy fluctuations often seen during manic episodes.

Hydration and Regular Eating Schedule:

Manic episodes can lead to neglecting basic bodily needs. Maintaining a regular eating schedule and prioritizing hydration can help ground you during times of heightened activity. Setting alarms or reminders to eat and drink water can be useful during these chaotic periods.

Mindful Eating Techniques:

During mania, practicing mindfulness at the table can help temper impulsivity. Taking a few deep breaths before eating, chewing slowly, and savoring each bite not only promotes better digestion but also allows you to remain connected to your body's true needs.

Supplements and Natural Remedies for Bipolar Wellness

While nutrition from whole foods is the cornerstone of managing bipolar disorder, supplements and natural remedies can offer additional support. It is essential to approach supplementation with care and to discuss any new additions with your healthcare provider, as interactions with medications can occur.

Omega-3 Supplements:

Omega-3 fatty acids are among the most researched supplements in relation to mood disorders. High-quality fish oil supplements, or plant-based alternatives like algae oil, can help fill nutritional gaps. These supplements may reduce inflammation, improve neuronal function, and contribute to overall mood stability.

B-Vitamin Complex:

B vitamins, particularly B6, B12, and folate, play a vital role in energy metabolism and neurotransmitter synthesis. For individuals with bipolar disorder, a B-vitamin complex supplement can support the conversion of food into energy and the production of mood-regulating neurotransmitters. This complex can be especially beneficial during periods when appetite is low or when dietary intake is insufficient.

Magnesium:

Magnesium is essential for a range of biochemical processes, including those that regulate nerve function and mood. Many people with bipolar disorder experience a deficiency in magnesium, which can lead to increased anxiety and mood instability. Magnesium supplements, or magnesium-rich natural remedies like Epsom salt baths, may help relax the nervous system and improve sleep quality.

Vitamin D:

A lack of vitamin D is widespread, particularly in areas with minimal sun exposure. Adequate levels of vitamin D have been linked to better mood regulation. In addition to safe sun exposure, vitamin D supplements can help maintain healthy levels, which is especially important during the darker months or for individuals who spend a lot of time indoors.

Herbal Remedies and Adaptogens:

Certain herbs and adaptogens have been traditionally used to support mental health. For example, ashwagandha is known for its stress-relieving properties, while St. John's Wort has been used to alleviate mild to moderate depressive symptoms. Other herbs, such as Rhodiola rosea, may help improve energy levels and mental clarity. It's important to note that herbal remedies should be used with caution and under the guidance of a healthcare provider, as they can interact with conventional medications.

Probiotics and Gut Health:

Emerging research underscores the connection between gut health and mental health. Probiotic supplements and fermented foods like yogurt, kefir, sauerkraut, and kimchi help support a healthy gut microbiome. A balanced microbiome can improve digestion, reduce inflammation, and positively influence mood through the gut-brain axis.

Amino Acid Supplements:

As the building blocks of neurotransmitters, amino acids like tryptophan and tyrosine are crucial for mood regulation. In certain cases, amino acid supplements may help bolster the production of serotonin and dopamine. However, these should be used carefully and ideally under medical supervision to ensure that they complement your overall treatment plan.

Mind-Body Therapies:

While not a supplement in the traditional sense, integrating mind-body therapies—such as meditation, yoga, and acupuncture—can amplify the effects of nutritional interventions and supplementation. These practices help reduce stress, promote relaxation, and improve overall emotional balance

Energizing Breakfasts for Stable Mornings

Omega-3 Power Oatmeal

Ingredients (1 serving):

½ cup rolled oats

1 cup unsweetened almond milk

1 tbsp ground flaxseeds

1 tbsp chia seeds

¼ cup blueberries

1 tbsp walnuts, chopped

½ tsp cinnamon

1 tsp honey (optional)

Instructions:

In a small pot, heat almond milk over medium heat.

Add oats and stir occasionally for 5 minutes until soft.

Stir in flaxseeds, chia seeds, and cinnamon.

Transfer to a bowl and top with blueberries, walnuts, and honey.

Nutritional Value (per serving):

Calories: 310

Protein: 8g

Carbs: 38g

Fiber: 9g

Fat: 14g

Omega-3s: 2.5g

Protein-Packed Scrambled Tofu

Ingredients (1 serving):

½ block (4 oz) firm tofu, crumbled

1 tsp olive oil

¼ tsp turmeric

¼ tsp black pepper

¼ tsp garlic powder

¼ tsp onion powder

¼ cup baby spinach

2 tbsp nutritional yeast

Instructions:

Warm olive oil in a pan over medium heat.

Add crumbled tofu and seasonings. Sauté for 3–5 minutes.

Stir in spinach and cook for 1 more minute.

Remove from heat and sprinkle with nutritional yeast.

Nutritional Value (per serving):

Calories: 250

Protein: 22g

Carbs: 7g

Fiber: 3g

Fat: 16g

Mood-Stabilizing Chia Pudding

Ingredients (1 serving):

3 tbsp chia seeds

1 cup unsweetened coconut milk

½ tsp vanilla extract

½ tsp cinnamon

1 tsp maple syrup

½ banana, sliced

1 tbsp hemp seeds

Instructions:

Mix chia seeds, coconut milk, vanilla, cinnamon, and maple syrup in a jar.

Mix thoroughly and chill in the refrigerator for a minimum of 4 hours or overnight.

Before serving, top with banana slices and hemp seeds.

Nutritional Value (per serving):

Calories: 320

Protein: 9g

Carbs: 28g

Fiber: 10g

Fat: 18g

Omega-3s: 3g

Blood Sugar-Stabilizing Avocado Toast

Ingredients (1 serving):

1 slice whole grain bread

½ avocado, mashed

1 tsp lemon juice

½ tsp red pepper flakes

1 boiled egg, sliced

Salt and pepper to taste

Instructions:

Toast bread until golden brown.

Mash avocado with lemon juice and spread over toast.

Top with boiled egg slices and red pepper flakes.

Season with salt and pepper.

Nutritional Value (per serving):

Calories: 290

Protein: 10g

Carbs: 24g

Fiber: 7g

Fat: 18g

Energizing Green Smoothie Bowl

Ingredients (1 serving):

1 cup spinach

½ frozen banana

½ cup unsweetened almond milk

1 tbsp almond butter

1 tbsp ground flaxseeds

½ tsp cinnamon

¼ cup granola (for topping)

Instructions:

Blend spinach, banana, almond milk, almond butter, flaxseeds, and cinnamon until smooth.

Pour into a bowl and top with granola.

Nutritional Value (per serving):

Calories: 330

Protein: 9g

Carbs: 35g

Fiber: 8g | Fat: 18g

Magnesium-Rich Quinoa Breakfast Bowl

Ingredients (1 serving):

½ cup cooked quinoa

½ cup unsweetened almond milk

1 tbsp pumpkin seeds

1 tbsp almonds, sliced

½ apple, diced

½ tsp cinnamon

1 tsp honey

Instructions:

Heat quinoa with almond milk over low heat for 3 minutes.

Stir in cinnamon, apple, and honey.

Top with pumpkin seeds and almonds.

Nutritional Value (per serving):

Calories: 310

Protein: 9g

Carbs: 40g

Fiber: 6g | Fat: 12g

Serotonin-Boosting Banana Walnut Pancakes

Ingredients (2 pancakes, 1 serving):

½ cup oat flour

½ ripe banana, mashed

½ tsp baking powder

1 egg

¼ cup unsweetened almond milk

1 tbsp walnuts, chopped

½ tsp cinnamon

1 tsp maple syrup

Instructions:

Mix oat flour, banana, baking powder, egg, almond milk, and cinnamon.

Heat a pan over medium heat and cook pancakes for 2–3 minutes per side.

Top with walnuts and drizzle with maple syrup.

Nutritional Value (per serving):

Calories: 320

Protein: 10g

Carbs: 42g

Fiber: 6g

Fat: 12g

Anti-Inflammatory Golden Latte with Protein

Ingredients (1 serving):

1 cup unsweetened coconut milk

½ tsp turmeric

½ tsp cinnamon

1 tbsp collagen powder

1 tsp honey

¼ tsp black pepper

Instructions:

Heat coconut milk in a saucepan.

Whisk in turmeric, cinnamon, collagen, honey, and black pepper.

Pour into a mug and enjoy warm.

Nutritional Value (per serving):

Calories: 140

Protein: 9g

Carbs: 9g

Fiber: 2g

Fat: 7g

Almond Butter & Berry Yogurt Parfait

Ingredients (1 serving):

½ cup Greek yogurt

1 tbsp almond butter

¼ cup mixed berries (strawberries, blueberries, raspberries)

2 tbsp granola

1 tsp honey

Instructions:

Layer Greek yogurt, almond butter, and berries in a cup.

Sprinkle with granola and drizzle with honey.

Nutritional Value (per serving):

Calories: 280

Protein: 15g

Carbs: 32g

Fiber: 6g

Fat: 10g

Balanced Blood Sugar Egg Muffins

Ingredients (3 muffins, 1 serving):

3 eggs

¼ cup spinach, chopped

¼ cup bell peppers, diced

2 tbsp feta cheese

1 tsp olive oil

Salt & pepper to taste

Instructions:

Preheat oven to 350°F (175°C).

Whisk eggs and mix with spinach, bell peppers, feta, salt, and pepper.

Grease a muffin tin with olive oil and pour in the mixture.

Bake for 15–18 minutes until set.

Nutritional Value (per serving):

Calories: 280

Protein: 21g

Carbs: 5g

Fiber: 1g | Fat: 18g

Mood-Stabilizing Lunches for Balanced Afternoons

Omega-3 Salmon & Quinoa Bowl

Ingredients (1 serving):

4 oz grilled salmon

½ cup cooked quinoa

½ avocado, sliced

½ cup steamed broccoli

1 tbsp pumpkin seeds

1 tbsp olive oil

1 tbsp lemon juice

Salt & pepper to taste

Instructions:

Grill salmon for 4–5 minutes per side until fully cooked.

Assemble a bowl with quinoa, broccoli, avocado, and salmon.

Drizzle with olive oil and lemon juice.

Sprinkle with pumpkin seeds, salt, and pepper.

Nutritional Value (per serving):

Calories: 480

Protein: 38g

Carbs: 28g

Fiber: 6g

Fat: 25g | Omega-3s: 2.8g

Lentil & Spinach Power Salad

Ingredients (1 serving):

½ cup cooked lentils

2 cups baby spinach

½ cup cherry tomatoes, halved

¼ cup cucumber, diced

2 tbsp crumbled feta cheese

1 tbsp olive oil

1 tbsp balsamic vinegar

1 tsp Dijon mustard

Instructions:

Toss all ingredients together in a bowl.

Drizzle with olive oil, balsamic vinegar, and Dijon mustard.

Nutritional Value (per serving):

Calories: 320

Protein: 18g

Carbs: 34g

Fiber: 9g | Fat: 14g

Turkey & Hummus Wrap

Ingredients (1 serving):

1 whole grain tortilla

3 oz sliced turkey breast

2 tbsp hummus

¼ avocado, sliced

¼ cup shredded carrots

½ cup mixed greens

Instructions:

Spread hummus on the tortilla.

Layer turkey, avocado, carrots, and greens.

Roll tightly and slice in half.

Nutritional Value (per serving):

Calories: 350

Protein: 28g

Carbs: 34g

Fiber: 7g

Fat: 12g

Blood Sugar-Stabilizing Chickpea & Avocado Toast

Ingredients (1 serving):

1 slice whole grain bread

½ avocado, mashed

¼ cup chickpeas, mashed

½ tsp lemon juice

¼ tsp cumin

Salt & pepper to taste

Instructions:

Toast the bread until crispy.

Mix mashed chickpeas with lemon juice, cumin, salt, and pepper.

Spread mashed avocado and chickpea mix over the toast.

Nutritional Value (per serving):

Calories: 290

Protein: 10g

Carbs: 35g

Fiber: 9g | Fat: 12g

Magnesium-Rich Quinoa & Roasted Veggie Bowl

Ingredients (1 serving):

½ cup cooked quinoa

½ cup roasted sweet potatoes

½ cup roasted Brussels sprouts

¼ cup cooked chickpeas

1 tbsp tahini dressing

Instructions:

Roast sweet potatoes and Brussels sprouts at 400°F for 20 minutes.

Mix quinoa, chickpeas, and roasted veggies in a bowl.

Drizzle with tahini dressing.

Nutritional Value (per serving):

Calories: 370

Protein: 14g

Carbs: 50g

Fiber: 10g

Fat: 12g

Mood-Boosting Tuna Salad Lettuce Wraps

Ingredients (1 serving):

1 can (3 oz) tuna, drained

1 tbsp Greek yogurt

½ tsp Dijon mustard

½ tsp lemon juice

1 tbsp chopped celery

1 tbsp chopped red onion

3 large lettuce leaves

Instructions:

Mix tuna, Greek yogurt, mustard, lemon juice, celery, and red onion.

Spoon the mixture into lettuce leaves and wrap.

Nutritional Value (per serving):

Calories: 230

Protein: 30g

Carbs: 6g

Fiber: 2g

Fat: 9g | Omega-3s: 1.5g

Stress-Reducing Miso Tofu Bowl

Ingredients (1 serving):

½ block (4 oz) firm tofu, cubed

½ cup cooked brown rice

½ cup steamed bok choy

1 tbsp miso paste

1 tsp sesame oil

½ tsp ginger, grated

Instructions:

Sauté tofu in sesame oil for 5 minutes.

Mix miso paste with a little warm water and drizzle over the tofu.

Serve with brown rice and bok choy.

Nutritional Value (per serving):

Calories: 350

Protein: 22g

Carbs: 38g

Fiber: 5g

Fat: 12g

Antioxidant-Rich Mediterranean Chickpea Salad

Ingredients (1 serving):

½ cup cooked chickpeas

½ cup cherry tomatoes, halved

¼ cup diced cucumber

2 tbsp crumbled feta cheese

1 tbsp olive oil

1 tbsp lemon juice

¼ tsp oregano

Instructions:

Toss all ingredients together in a bowl.

Drizzle with olive oil and lemon juice.

Nutritional Value (per serving):

Calories: 320

Protein: 12g

Carbs: 38g

Fiber: 8g | Fat: 14g

Balancing Blood Sugar Lentil Soup

Ingredients (1 serving):

½ cup cooked lentils

1 cup vegetable broth

¼ cup diced carrots

¼ cup diced celery

½ tsp cumin

1 tbsp olive oil

Instructions:

Sauté carrots and celery in olive oil for 5 minutes.

Add lentils, broth, and cumin. Simmer for 10 minutes.

Nutritional Value (per serving):

Calories: 290

Protein: 15g

Carbs: 35g

Fiber: 9g

Fat: 8g

Serotonin-Boosting Grilled Chicken & Avocado Salad

Ingredients (1 serving):

4 oz grilled chicken breast

2 cups mixed greens

½ avocado, sliced

¼ cup cherry tomatoes

1 tbsp olive oil

1 tbsp balsamic vinegar

Instructions:

Cook the chicken on the grill for 5–6 minutes per side until thoroughly done.

Toss greens, tomatoes, and avocado in a bowl.

Slice chicken and add to the salad.

Drizzle with olive oil and balsamic vinegar.

Nutritional Value (per serving):

Calories: 400

Protein: 40g

Carbs: 12g

Fiber: 6g

Fat: 22g

Grounding Dinners for Restful Evenings

Magnesium-Rich Baked Salmon with Quinoa & Roasted Vegetables

Ingredients (1 serving):

4 oz salmon fillet

½ cup cooked quinoa

½ cup roasted sweet potatoes

½ cup steamed kale

1 tbsp olive oil

1 tbsp lemon juice

½ tsp garlic powder

½ tsp turmeric

Salt & pepper to taste

Instructions:

Preheat oven to 375°F (190°C).

Rub salmon with olive oil, garlic powder, turmeric, salt, and pepper.

Bake for 15–18 minutes.

Roast sweet potatoes at 375°F for 25 minutes.

Serve with quinoa and steamed kale. Drizzle with lemon juice.

Nutritional Value (per serving):

Calories: 520 | Protein: 42g

Carbs: 42g | Fiber: 7g

Fat: 22g | Omega-3s: 2.5g

Sleep-Promoting Turkey & Brown Rice Bowl

Ingredients (1 serving):

4 oz ground turkey

½ cup cooked brown rice

½ cup sautéed spinach

1 tbsp olive oil

½ tsp cumin

½ tsp paprika

½ tsp garlic powder

Salt & pepper to taste

Instructions:

Cook ground turkey in olive oil over medium heat, adding spices.

Serve over brown rice with sautéed spinach.

Nutritional Value (per serving):

Calories: 460

Protein: 40g

Carbs: 44g

Fiber: 5g | Fat: 14g

Calming Lentil & Vegetable Stew

Ingredients (1 serving):

½ cup cooked lentils

1 cup vegetable broth

½ cup chopped carrots

½ cup diced zucchini

1 tbsp olive oil

½ tsp cumin

½ tsp turmeric

½ tsp thyme

Instructions:

Sauté carrots and zucchini in olive oil for 5 minutes.

Add lentils, broth, and spices. Simmer for 15 minutes.

Nutritional Value (per serving):

Calories: 370

Protein: 18g

Carbs: 48g

Fiber: 12g | Fat: 10g

Grounding Baked Cod with Mashed Sweet Potatoes

Ingredients (1 serving):

4 oz cod fillet

½ cup mashed sweet potatoes

½ cup steamed broccoli

1 tbsp olive oil

½ tsp paprika

½ tsp garlic powder

½ tsp lemon zest

Instructions:

Preheat oven to 375°F.

Season cod with paprika, garlic powder, and lemon zest. Bake for 15 minutes.

Mash sweet potatoes with olive oil. Serve with cod and steamed broccoli.

Nutritional Value (per serving):

Calories: 420

Protein: 36g

Carbs: 45g

Fiber: 8g

Fat: 12g

Tryptophan-Boosting Chicken & Chickpea Stir-Fry

Ingredients (1 serving):

4 oz chicken breast, cubed

½ cup cooked chickpeas

½ cup sautéed bell peppers

1 tbsp coconut oil

½ tsp ginger

½ tsp garlic

1 tbsp tamari sauce

Instructions:

Sauté chicken in coconut oil for 5 minutes.

Add chickpeas, bell peppers, ginger, and garlic. Cook for another 5 minutes.

Drizzle with tamari sauce and serve.

Nutritional Value (per serving):

Calories: 460

Protein: 42g

Carbs: 38g

Fiber: 8g

Fat: 16g

Serotonin-Boosting Wild Rice & Mushroom Bowl

Ingredients (1 serving):

½ cup cooked wild rice

½ cup sautéed mushrooms

½ cup steamed asparagus

1 tbsp olive oil

1 tbsp tahini

½ tsp black pepper

Instructions:

Cook wild rice according to package instructions.

Sauté mushrooms in olive oil.

Assemble rice, mushrooms, and asparagus in a bowl. Drizzle with tahini.

Nutritional Value (per serving):

Calories: 390

Protein: 14g

Carbs: 48g

Fiber: 8g | Fat: 14g

Zinc-Rich Beef & Roasted Root Vegetables

Ingredients (1 serving):

4 oz grass-fed beef steak

½ cup roasted carrots

½ cup roasted parsnips

1 tbsp olive oil

½ tsp rosemary

½ tsp sea salt

Instructions:

Roast carrots and parsnips at 375°F for 25 minutes.

Grill beef for 4–5 minutes per side.

Serve together with a drizzle of olive oil.

Nutritional Value (per serving):

Calories: 480

Protein: 45g

Carbs: 36g

Fiber: 6g

Fat: 16g

Omega-3-Rich Sardine & Spinach Pasta

Ingredients (1 serving):

½ cup whole grain pasta

1 can (3 oz) sardines

½ cup sautéed spinach

1 tbsp olive oil

½ tsp garlic powder

½ tsp lemon juice

Instructions:

Cook pasta according to package instructions.

Sauté spinach in olive oil and mix with pasta.

Add sardines and drizzle with lemon juice.

Nutritional Value (per serving):

Calories: 420

Protein: 35g

Carbs: 40g

Fiber: 7g

Fat: 14g | Omega-3s: 2.3g

Balancing Chickpea & Avocado Buddha Bowl

Ingredients (1 serving):

½ cup cooked quinoa

½ cup chickpeas

½ avocado, sliced

½ cup steamed kale

1 tbsp olive oil

½ tsp turmeric

½ tsp black pepper

Instructions:

Assemble all ingredients in a bowl.

Lightly coat with olive oil and season with turmeric and black pepper.

Nutritional Value (per serving):

Calories: 460

Protein: 18g

Carbs: 50g

Fiber: 11g

Fat: 20g

Cortisol-Lowering Baked Tempeh & Brown Rice Bowl

Ingredients (1 serving):

½ block (4 oz) tempeh

½ cup cooked brown rice

½ cup roasted Brussels sprouts

1 tbsp tamari sauce

1 tsp sesame seeds

1 tbsp coconut oil

Instructions:

Bake tempeh at 375°F for 20 minutes.

Roast Brussels sprouts in coconut oil.

Serve tempeh and Brussels sprouts over brown rice. Drizzle with tamari sauce and sprinkle sesame seeds on top.

Nutritional Value (per serving):

Calories: 480

Protein: 32g

Carbs: 42g

Fiber: 8g

Fat: 18g

Smart Snacks for Energy Without the Crash

Omega-3 Power Trail Mix

Ingredients (1 serving):

¼ cup walnuts

2 tbsp pumpkin seeds

2 tbsp dark chocolate chips (70% or higher)

2 tbsp dried blueberries

1 tbsp flaxseeds

Instructions:

Mix all ingredients in a bowl.

Store in an airtight container for snacking.

Nutritional Value (per serving):

Calories: 320

Protein: 8g

Carbs: 24g

Fiber: 5g

Fat: 24g

Omega-3s: 2.1g

Protein-Packed Greek Yogurt & Berry Bowl

Ingredients (1 serving):

½ cup plain Greek yogurt

¼ cup mixed berries (blueberries, raspberries, strawberries)

1 tbsp chia seeds

1 tsp honey

Instructions:

Mix Greek yogurt with berries and chia seeds.

Drizzle with honey before serving.

Nutritional Value (per serving):

Calories: 220

Protein: 16g

Carbs: 28g

Fiber: 6g

Fat: 4g

Almond Butter & Banana Energy Bites

Ingredients (1 serving, 3 bites):

½ banana, mashed

2 tbsp almond butter

¼ cup rolled oats

1 tbsp flaxseeds

½ tsp cinnamon

Instructions:

Mix all ingredients in a bowl.

Form into small bite-sized balls.

Refrigerate for 30 minutes before eating.

Nutritional Value (per serving):

Calories: 250

Protein: 8g

Carbs: 28g

Fiber: 5g

Fat: 12g

Hard-Boiled Eggs with Avocado Slices

Ingredients (1 serving):

2 hard-boiled eggs

¼ avocado, sliced

½ tsp sea salt

½ tsp black pepper

Instructions:

Slice the eggs and avocado.

Sprinkle with salt and pepper before eating.

Nutritional Value (per serving):

Calories: 280

Protein: 18g

Carbs: 6g

Fiber: 3g

Fat: 22g

Hummus & Veggie Sticks

Ingredients (1 serving):

¼ cup hummus

½ cup sliced cucumbers

½ cup baby carrots

½ cup bell pepper strips

Instructions:

Serve hummus with sliced vegetables for dipping.

Nutritional Value (per serving):

Calories: 200

Protein: 8g

Carbs: 26g

Fiber: 7g

Fat: 8g

Chia Seed Pudding with Coconut Milk

Ingredients (1 serving):

2 tbsp chia seeds

½ cup unsweetened coconut milk

½ tsp vanilla extract

1 tsp maple syrup

Instructions:

Mix all ingredients in a bowl.

Refrigerate for at least 2 hours or overnight.

Nutritional Value (per serving):

Calories: 210

Protein: 6g

Carbs: 16g

Fiber: 10g

Fat: 14g

Dark Chocolate & Almond Butter Rice Cakes

Ingredients (1 serving):

1 brown rice cake

1 tbsp almond butter

1 square (10g) dark chocolate (85%)

Instructions:

Spread almond butter on the rice cake.

Melt the dark chocolate and drizzle on top.

Nutritional Value (per serving):

Calories: 230

Protein: 5g

Carbs: 20g

Fiber: 4g

Fat: 14g

Roasted Chickpeas with Spices

Ingredients (1 serving):

½ cup cooked chickpeas

1 tsp olive oil

½ tsp smoked paprika

½ tsp garlic powder

½ tsp sea salt

Instructions:

Toss chickpeas with olive oil and spices.

Roast at 375°F (190°C) for 20 minutes.

Nutritional Value (per serving):

Calories: 180

Protein: 8g

Carbs: 26g

Fiber: 6g

Fat: 5g

Cottage Cheese & Pineapple Bowl

Ingredients (1 serving):

½ cup cottage cheese

¼ cup diced pineapple

1 tbsp pumpkin seeds

Instructions:

Mix all ingredients in a bowl.

Nutritional Value (per serving):

Calories: 220

Protein: 18g

Carbs: 20g

Fiber: 3g

Fat: 6g

Edamame with Sea Salt & Lemon

Ingredients (1 serving):

½ cup steamed edamame

½ tsp sea salt

½ tsp lemon juice

Instructions:

Steam edamame for 5 minutes.

Sprinkle with salt and lemon juice before eating.

Nutritional Value (per serving):

Calories: 190

Protein: 16g

Carbs: 15g

Fiber: 6g

Fat: 8g

Healing Herbal Teas and Mood-Boosting Beverages

Calming Chamomile & Lavender Tea

Ingredients (1 serving):

1 cup hot water (8 oz)

1 tsp dried chamomile flowers

½ tsp dried lavender

1 tsp raw honey (optional)

Instructions:

Steep chamomile and lavender in hot water for 5 minutes.

Strain and add honey if desired.

Nutritional Value (per serving):

Calories: 15 (without honey), 40 (with honey)

Carbs: 10g (with honey)

Fat: 0g

Protein: 0g

Benefits: **Reduces stress, improves sleep, calms nervous system**

Ashwagandha & Turmeric Golden Milk

Ingredients (1 serving):

1 cup unsweetened almond milk

½ tsp ashwagandha powder

½ tsp turmeric powder

¼ tsp cinnamon

1 tsp raw honey

½ tsp coconut oil

Instructions:

Heat almond milk over low heat.

Stir in ashwagandha, turmeric, cinnamon, and coconut oil.

Remove from heat and mix in honey.

Nutritional Value (per serving):

Calories: 90

Protein: 1g

Carbs: 10g

Fat: 4g

Benefits: **Reduces anxiety, balances cortisol, supports brain health**

Lemon Balm & Peppermint Mood Tea

Ingredients (1 serving):

1 cup hot water (8 oz)

1 tsp dried lemon balm

½ tsp dried peppermint leaves

1 tsp lemon juice

Instructions:

Steep lemon balm and peppermint in hot water for 5 minutes.

Strain and add lemon juice before drinking.

Nutritional Value (per serving):

Calories: 5

Carbs: 1g

Fat: 0g

Protein: 0g

Benefits: **Reduces nervous tension, aids digestion, refreshes the mind**

Magnesium-Rich Cacao Bliss Drink

Ingredients (1 serving):

1 cup unsweetened oat milk

1 tbsp raw cacao powder

1 tsp coconut sugar

¼ tsp cinnamon

Instructions:

Heat oat milk over low heat.

Stir in cacao, coconut sugar, and cinnamon.

Whisk until smooth.

Nutritional Value (per serving):

Calories: 120

Protein: 2g

Carbs: 18g

Fat: 4g

Benefits: **Boosts serotonin, provides magnesium, enhances relaxation**

Adaptogenic Rhodiola & Rose Tea

Ingredients (1 serving):

1 cup hot water (8 oz)

½ tsp dried rhodiola root

1 tsp dried rose petals

Instructions:

Steep rhodiola and rose petals in hot water for 5–7 minutes.

Strain and drink warm.

Nutritional Value (per serving):

Calories: 5

Carbs: 1g

Fat: 0g

Protein: 0g

Benefits: **Improves focus, enhances mood stability, combats fatigue**

Anti-Inflammatory Ginger & Lemon Tea

Ingredients (1 serving):

1 cup hot water (8 oz)

1 tsp freshly grated ginger

1 tsp lemon juice

½ tsp raw honey

Instructions:

Steep ginger in hot water for 5 minutes.

Strain and add lemon juice and honey.

Nutritional Value (per serving):

Calories: 30

Carbs: 8g

Fat: 0g

Protein: 0g

Benefits: **Supports digestion, reduces inflammation, stabilizes energy levels**

Serotonin-Boosting Matcha Latte

Ingredients (1 serving):

1 cup unsweetened almond milk

1 tsp matcha powder

½ tsp vanilla extract

1 tsp maple syrup

Instructions:

Heat almond milk over low heat.

Whisk in matcha powder, vanilla, and maple syrup.

Nutritional Value (per serving):

Calories: 80

Protein: 2g

Carbs: 12g

Fat: 2g

Benefits: **Boosts dopamine, enhances mental clarity, stabilizes mood**

Maca & Banana Mood Smoothie

Ingredients (1 serving):

1 banana

1 tsp maca powder

1 cup unsweetened almond milk

½ tsp cinnamon

1 tsp honey

Instructions:

Blend all ingredients until smooth.

Nutritional Value (per serving):

Calories: 180

Protein: 3g

Carbs: 38g

Fat: 2g

Benefits: **Balances hormones, boosts energy, reduces anxiety**

Calming Valerian & Passionflower Night Tea

Ingredients (1 serving):

1 cup hot water (8 oz)

½ tsp valerian root

½ tsp dried passionflower

Instructions:

Steep valerian and passionflower in hot water for 10 minutes.

Strain before drinking.

Nutritional Value (per serving):

Calories: 5

Carbs: 1g

Fat: 0g

Protein: 0g

Benefits: **Promotes deep sleep, reduces restlessness, calms the nervous system**

Blueberry & Flax Brain-Boost Smoothie

Ingredients (1 serving):

½ cup frozen blueberries

1 tbsp ground flaxseeds

1 cup unsweetened coconut milk

½ tsp vanilla extract

Instructions:

Blend all ingredients until smooth.

Nutritional Value (per serving):

Calories: 140

Protein: 3g

Carbs: 18g

Fat: 6g

Benefits: **Supports brain health, provides antioxidants, stabilizes energy**

Comforting Soups and Stews for Emotional Nourishment

Mood-Boosting Lentil & Turmeric Soup

Ingredients (4 servings):

1 cup red lentils, rinsed

4 cups vegetable broth

1 tablespoon of olive oil | 1 small chopped onion

2 cloves garlic, minced

1 tsp turmeric powder

½ tsp cumin

1 carrot, diced

½ tsp black pepper

Juice of ½ lemon

Instructions:

Warm olive oil in a pot, then sauté the onion and garlic until they become translucent.

Add turmeric, cumin, and black pepper. Stir for 30 seconds.

Add carrots, lentils, and vegetable broth. Simmer for 20 minutes.

Blend for a creamy texture or leave chunky. Stir in lemon juice before serving.

Nutritional Value (per serving):

Calories: 180 | Protein: 12g

Carbs: 30g | Fat: 4g

Benefits: **Rich in protein, stabilizes blood sugar, supports brain health**

Gut-Healing Miso & Mushroom Soup

Ingredients (4 servings):

4 cups water

3 tbsp miso paste

1 cup shiitake mushrooms, sliced

1 cup tofu, cubed

2 green onions, chopped

½ tsp grated ginger

Instructions:

Heat water in a pot, add mushrooms and ginger. Simmer for 10 minutes.

Take off the heat and mix in the miso paste until fully dissolved.

Add tofu and green onions before serving.

Nutritional Value (per serving):

Calories: 120

Protein: 9g

Carbs: 12g

Fat: 4g

Benefits: **Supports gut health, provides probiotics, aids digestion**

Omega-3 Rich Salmon & Spinach Chowder

Ingredients (4 servings):

1 tbsp olive oil

1 small onion, chopped

2 cloves garlic, minced

4 cups vegetable broth

1 cup coconut milk

1 salmon fillet (6 oz), cut into chunks

2 cups fresh spinach

½ tsp black pepper

½ tsp thyme

Instructions:

Warm olive oil in a pan, then sauté the onion and garlic until tender.

Add broth, coconut milk, thyme, and black pepper. Simmer for 10 minutes.

Add salmon chunks, cook for 5 minutes.

Stir in spinach and remove from heat.

Nutritional Value (per serving):

Calories: 250

Protein: 20g

Carbs: 10g | Fat: 15g

Benefits: **Rich in omega-3s, reduces inflammation, supports cognitive function**

Calming Sweet Potato & Coconut Soup

Ingredients (4 servings):

2 medium sweet potatoes, peeled and diced

4 cups vegetable broth

1 cup coconut milk

1 tbsp olive oil

½ tsp cinnamon

½ tsp turmeric

1 small onion, chopped

Instructions:

Heat olive oil, sauté onion until soft.

Add sweet potatoes, broth, turmeric, and cinnamon. Simmer for 20 minutes.

Blend until smooth, then stir in coconut milk before serving.

Nutritional Value (per serving):

Calories: 220

Protein: 3g

Carbs: 35g

Fat: 9g

Benefits: **Supports serotonin production, reduces inflammation, provides stable energy**

Magnesium-Rich Black Bean & Kale Soup

Ingredients (4 servings):

1 tbsp olive oil

1 small onion, chopped

2 cloves garlic, minced

1 can black beans, drained

4 cups vegetable broth

2 cups kale, chopped

½ tsp cumin

Juice of ½ lime

Instructions:

Warm olive oil in a pan and cook the onion and garlic until they soften.

Add black beans, broth, and cumin. Simmer for 15 minutes.

Stir in kale and cook for 5 more minutes. Add lime juice before serving.

Nutritional Value (per serving):

Calories: 180

Protein: 10g

Carbs: 28g

Fat: 4g

Benefits: **Rich in magnesium, improves sleep, reduces anxiety**

Anti-Inflammatory Carrot & Ginger Soup

Ingredients (4 servings):

4 large carrots, chopped

4 cups vegetable broth

1 small onion, chopped

1 tsp grated ginger

1 tbsp olive oil

Instructions:

Heat olive oil, sauté onion and ginger.

Add carrots and broth. Simmer for 20 minutes.

Blend until smooth before serving.

Nutritional Value (per serving):

Calories: 150

Protein: 2g

Carbs: 30g

Fat: 5g

Benefits: **Reduces inflammation, stabilizes mood, supports digestion**

Protein-Packed Chickpea & Spinach Stew

Ingredients (4 servings):

1 tbsp olive oil

1 small onion, chopped

2 cloves garlic, minced

1 can chickpeas, drained

4 cups vegetable broth

2 cups spinach

½ tsp cumin

Instructions:

Sauté onion and garlic in olive oil.

Add chickpeas, broth, and cumin. Simmer for 15 minutes.

Stir in spinach before serving.

Nutritional Value (per serving):

Calories: 210

Protein: 12g

Carbs: 30g

Fat: 6g

Benefits: **Rich in plant-based protein, stabilizes blood sugar, supports neurotransmitters**

Zinc-Boosting Lentil & Mushroom Stew

Ingredients (4 servings):

1 cup green lentils

4 cups vegetable broth

1 cup mushrooms, sliced

1 tbsp olive oil

½ tsp thyme

Instructions:

Sauté mushrooms in olive oil.

Add lentils, broth, and thyme. Simmer for 20 minutes.

Nutritional Value (per serving):

Calories: 190

Protein: 14g

Carbs: 30g

Fat: 3g

Benefits: **Rich in zinc, improves cognition, boosts immune function**

Adaptogenic Shiitake & Barley Soup

Ingredients (4 servings):

1 tbsp olive oil

1 small onion, chopped

1 cup shiitake mushrooms, sliced

½ cup barley

4 cups vegetable broth

½ tsp black pepper

Instructions:

Sauté onion and mushrooms in olive oil.

Add barley, broth, and black pepper. Simmer for 25 minutes.

Nutritional Value (per serving):

Calories: 220

Protein: 8g

Carbs: 40g

Fat: 3g

Benefits: **Supports adrenal function, balances stress hormones**

Bone-Building Broccoli & Almond Soup

Ingredients (4 servings):

2 cups broccoli florets

4 cups vegetable broth

1 tbsp almond butter

½ tsp garlic powder

Instructions:

Cook broccoli in broth until tender.

Blend with almond butter and garlic powder.

Nutritional Value (per serving):

Calories: 180

Protein: 7g

Carbs: 18g

Fat: 9g

Benefits: **Supports bone health, reduces stress, stabilizes mood**

Gut-Healthy and Anti-Inflammatory Recipe

Probiotic-Rich Coconut Yogurt Bowl

Ingredients (1 serving):

½ cup unsweetened coconut yogurt

¼ cup blueberries

1 tbsp chia seeds

1 tbsp walnuts, chopped

½ tsp cinnamon

Instructions:

In a bowl, mix coconut yogurt with cinnamon.

Top with blueberries, chia seeds, and walnuts.

Nutritional Value:

Calories: 210

Protein: 5g

Carbs: 18g

Fat: 14g

Benefits: Rich in probiotics, supports gut microbiome, reduces inflammation

Turmeric & Ginger Smoothie

Ingredients (1 serving):

1 cup unsweetened almond milk

1 banana

½ tsp turmeric powder

½ tsp grated ginger

1 tbsp flaxseeds

Instructions:

Blend all ingredients until smooth.

Nutritional Value:

Calories: 180

Protein: 4g

Carbs: 28g

Fat: 6g

Benefits: Anti-inflammatory, supports digestion, reduces brain fog

Gut-Healing Bone Broth Soup

Ingredients (4 servings):

4 cups bone broth

1 cup chopped carrots

1 cup kale, chopped

1 tsp apple cider vinegar

½ tsp turmeric

Instructions:

Heat bone broth in a pot, add carrots and turmeric. Simmer for 15 minutes.

Stir in kale and apple cider vinegar before serving.

Nutritional Value (per serving):

Calories: 150

Protein: 10g

Carbs: 12g

Fat: 6g

Benefits: Supports gut lining, reduces inflammation, balances neurotransmitters

Fermented Kimchi Avocado Toast

Ingredients (1 serving):

1 slice whole-grain sourdough bread

½ avocado, mashed

2 tbsp kimchi

Instructions:

Toast bread and spread mashed avocado.

Top with kimchi before serving.

Nutritional Value:

Calories: 220

Protein: 6g

Carbs: 28g

Fat: 10g

Benefits: Rich in probiotics, supports serotonin production

Anti-Inflammatory Golden Milk Latte

Ingredients (1 serving):

1 cup coconut milk

½ tsp turmeric

½ tsp cinnamon

½ tsp grated ginger

1 tsp honey

Instructions:

Heat coconut milk, stir in turmeric, cinnamon, and ginger.

Sweeten with honey before serving.

Nutritional Value:

Calories: 180

Protein: 2g

Carbs: 15g

Fat: 12g

Benefits: Calms nervous system, reduces inflammation

Prebiotic Roasted Garlic & Leek Soup

Ingredients (4 servings):

1 head garlic, roasted

1 leek, sliced

4 cups vegetable broth

1 tbsp olive oil

Instructions:

Sauté leeks in olive oil, add roasted garlic and broth. Simmer for 15 minutes.

Blend until smooth before serving.

Nutritional Value (per serving):

Calories: 160

Protein: 3g

Carbs: 20g

Fat: 8g

Benefits: Feeds good gut bacteria, enhances brain function

Omega-3 Rich Chia Pudding

Ingredients (1 serving):

½ cup unsweetened almond milk

2 tbsp chia seeds

½ tsp cinnamon

½ tsp vanilla extract

Instructions:

Mix ingredients and refrigerate for 4 hours until thick.

Nutritional Value:

Calories: 180

Protein: 5g

Carbs: 14g

Fat: 10g

Benefits: Supports gut health, balances mood

Detoxifying Beet & Ginger Salad

Ingredients (2 servings):

2 medium beets, grated

1 tbsp apple cider vinegar

1 tbsp olive oil

½ tsp grated ginger

Instructions:

Mix all ingredients in a bowl. Let sit for 10 minutes before serving.

Nutritional Value (per serving):

Calories: 120

Protein: 2g

Carbs: 15g

Fat: 6g

Benefits: Supports liver detox, reduces oxidative stress

Gut-Soothing Papaya & Coconut Bowl

Ingredients (1 serving):

1 cup papaya, chopped

½ cup unsweetened coconut yogurt

1 tbsp shredded coconut

Instructions:

Mix all ingredients in a bowl.

Nutritional Value:

Calories: 190

Protein: 3g

Carbs: 28g

Fat: 8g

Benefits: Aids digestion, reduces bloating, calms gut inflammation

Anti-Anxiety Almond & Blueberry Smoothie

Ingredients (1 serving):

1 cup unsweetened almond milk

½ cup blueberries

1 tbsp almond butter

½ tsp cinnamon

Instructions:

Blend all ingredients until smooth.

Nutritional Value:

Calories: 220

Protein: 6g

Carbs: 22g

Fat: 12g

Benefits: Supports brain function, stabilizes blood sugar, reduces stress

Bonus: 28-Day Bipolar-Friendly Meal Plan

Day 1 to Day 7

Day 1

Breakfast: Probiotic-Rich Coconut Yogurt Bowl

Lunch: Lentil & Quinoa Buddha Bowl

Dinner: Magnesium-Rich Spinach & Chickpea Stew

Snack: Dark Chocolate Almond Energy Bites

Beverage: Anti-Inflammatory Golden Milk Latte

Day 2

Breakfast: Turmeric & Ginger Smoothie

Lunch: Avocado & Hummus Wrap

Dinner: Omega-3 Salmon with Roasted Sweet Potatoes

Snack: Walnuts & Blueberries

Beverage: Gut-Soothing Papaya & Coconut Bowl

Day 3

Breakfast: Overnight Chia & Flax Pudding

Lunch: Detoxifying Beet & Ginger Salad

Dinner: Turkey & Zucchini Stir-Fry

Snack: Fermented Kimchi Avocado Toast

Beverage: Stress-Relief Chamomile Tea

Day 4

Breakfast: Almond & Blueberry Smoothie

Lunch: Mediterranean Chickpea Salad

Dinner: Comforting Butternut Squash & Lentil Soup

Snack: Pumpkin Seeds & Dark Chocolate

Beverage: Ginger & Lemon Tea

Day 5

Breakfast: Gut-Healing Bone Broth Soup

Lunch: Prebiotic Roasted Garlic & Leek Soup

Dinner: Slow-Cooked Turmeric Chicken & Brown Rice

Snack: Homemade Trail Mix (Walnuts, Pumpkin Seeds, Coconut Flakes)

Beverage: Hibiscus & Mint Tea

Day 6

Breakfast: Scrambled Eggs with Spinach & Avocado

Lunch: Wild Rice & Roasted Veggie Bowl

Dinner: Miso Soup with Tofu & Mushrooms

Snack: Apple Slices with Almond Butter

Beverage: Lemon Balm & Lavender Tea

Day 7

Breakfast: Berry & Coconut Smoothie Bowl

Lunch: Quinoa & Roasted Cauliflower Salad

Dinner: Hearty Lentil & Kale Soup

Snack: Dark Chocolate & Walnut Clusters

Beverage: Digestive Fennel & Peppermint Tea

Day 8 to Day 14

Day 8

Breakfast: Omega-3 Rich Chia Pudding

Lunch: Sautéed Greens & Quinoa Bowl

Dinner: Slow-Cooked Salmon & Steamed Vegetables

Snack: Mixed Nuts & Coconut Chips

Beverage: Ashwagandha & Cinnamon Tea

Day 9

Breakfast: Probiotic-Rich Coconut Yogurt Bowl

Lunch: Lentil & Roasted Veggie Wrap

Dinner: Garlic & Herb Baked Chicken with Brown Rice

Snack: Blueberry & Almond Butter Bites

Beverage: Chamomile & Honey Tea

Day 10

Breakfast: Gut-Healing Bone Broth Soup

Lunch: Avocado & Hummus Wrap

Dinner: Butternut Squash & Lentil Soup

Snack: Pumpkin Seeds & Dark Chocolate

Beverage: Hibiscus & Mint Tea

Day 11

Breakfast: Turmeric & Ginger Smoothie

Lunch: Mediterranean Chickpea & Quinoa Salad

Dinner: Baked Salmon with Steamed Broccoli & Sweet Potato Mash

Snack: Dark Chocolate Almond Energy Bites

Beverage: Stress-Relief Chamomile Tea

Day 12

Breakfast: Scrambled Eggs with Spinach & Avocado

Lunch: Sautéed Greens with Wild Rice & Tahini Dressing

Dinner: Hearty Lentil & Kale Soup

Snack: Apple Slices with Almond Butter

Beverage: Anti-Inflammatory Ginger & Lemon Tea

Day 13

Breakfast: Berry & Coconut Smoothie Bowl

Lunch: Avocado & Hummus Wrap with Fresh Greens

Dinner: Slow-Cooked Turmeric Chicken with Brown Rice

Snack: Pumpkin Seeds & Coconut Flakes

Beverage: Ashwagandha & Cinnamon Tea

Day 14

Breakfast: Gut-Healing Bone Broth with Miso & Mushrooms

Lunch: Roasted Cauliflower & Quinoa Bowl

Dinner: Garlic & Herb Baked Chicken with Steamed Asparagus

Snack: Blueberry & Almond Butter Bites

Beverage: Digestive Fennel & Peppermint Tea

Day 15 to Day 21

Day 15

Breakfast: Chia & Flax Overnight Pudding

Lunch: Wild Rice & Roasted Veggie Bowl

Dinner: Tofu and Shiitake Mushroom Miso Soup

Snack: Homemade Trail Mix (Walnuts, Pumpkin Seeds, Coconut Chips)

Beverage: Hibiscus & Mint Tea

Day 16

Breakfast: Probiotic-Rich Coconut Yogurt with Berries

Lunch: Lentil & Roasted Veggie Wrap

Dinner: Butternut Squash & Red Lentil Stew

Snack: Dark Chocolate & Walnut Clusters

Beverage: Lemon Balm & Lavender Tea

Day 17

Breakfast: Omega-3 Rich Chia Pudding with Almonds

Lunch: Sautéed Greens with Chickpeas & Tahini

Dinner: Grilled Salmon with Quinoa & Roasted Peppers

Snack: Mixed Nuts & Coconut Chips

Beverage: Chamomile & Honey Tea

Day 18

Breakfast: Spinach & Mushroom Scrambled Eggs

Lunch: Detoxifying Beet & Ginger Salad

Dinner: Comforting Turmeric Lentil Soup

Snack: Fermented Kimchi Avocado Toast

Beverage: Lemon & Ginger Tea

Day 19

Breakfast: Almond & Blueberry Smoothie

Lunch: Roasted Sweet Potato & Quinoa Salad

Dinner: Slow-Cooked Chicken & Root Vegetables

Snack: Pumpkin Seeds & Dark Chocolate

Beverage: Soothing Peppermint & Lavender Tea

Day 20

Breakfast: Gut-Healing Bone Broth Soup

Lunch: Mediterranean Chickpea Salad

Dinner: Omega-3 Baked Trout with Steamed Kale

Snack: Walnuts & Blueberries

Beverage: Ashwagandha & Cinnamon Latte

Day 21

Breakfast: Probiotic Greek Yogurt with Ground Flaxseeds

Lunch: Sautéed Greens & Lentils with Lemon Dressing

Dinner: Mushroom & Herb Risotto with Brown Rice

Snack: Homemade Energy Bars (Dates, Nuts, Seeds)

Beverage: Digestive Fennel & Mint Tea

Day 22 to Day 28

Day 22

Breakfast: Chia & Almond Overnight Pudding

Lunch: Avocado & Hummus Wrap

Dinner: Garlic & Lemon Chicken with Wild Rice

Snack: Apple Slices with Nut Butter

Beverage: Stress-Relief Chamomile Tea

Day 23

Breakfast: Turmeric & Ginger Smoothie

Lunch: Lentil & Roasted Veggie Bowl

Dinner: Miso Soup with Bok Choy & Mushrooms

Snack: Pumpkin Seeds & Coconut Flakes

Beverage: Hibiscus & Mint Tea

Day 24

Breakfast: Scrambled Eggs with Spinach & Avocado

Lunch: Wild Rice & Roasted Cauliflower Salad

Dinner: Slow-Cooked Turmeric Chicken with Brown Rice

Snack: Blueberry & Almond Butter Bites

Beverage: Anti-Inflammatory Ginger & Lemon Tea

Day 25

Breakfast: Berry & Coconut Smoothie Bowl

Lunch: Detoxifying Beet & Ginger Salad

Dinner: Grilled Salmon with Steamed Broccoli & Quinoa

Snack: Dark Chocolate & Walnut Clusters

Beverage: Ashwagandha & Cinnamon Latte

Day 26

Breakfast: Probiotic Greek Yogurt with Ground Flaxseeds

Lunch: Sautéed Greens & Chickpeas with Tahini

Dinner: Comforting Butternut Squash & Red Lentil Soup

Snack: Fermented Kimchi Avocado Toast

Beverage: Soothing Peppermint & Lavender Tea

Day 27

Breakfast: Omega-3 Rich Chia Pudding with Almonds

Lunch: Roasted Sweet Potato & Quinoa Salad

Dinner: Garlic & Herb Baked Chicken with Roasted Vegetables

Snack: Mixed Nuts & Coconut Chips

Beverage: Chamomile & Honey Tea

Day 28

Breakfast: Gut-Healing Bone Broth with Miso & Mushrooms

Lunch: Mediterranean Chickpea & Quinoa Salad

Dinner: Hearty Lentil & Kale Soup

Snack: Dark Chocolate & Almond Energy Bites

Beverage: Digestive Fennel & Mint Tea

Conclusion

Nourishing Stability, Empowering Wellness

Bipolar disorder is a journey—one of highs and lows, of challenges and resilience. But through this cookbook, we have explored the undeniable connection between **nutrition and mental stability**, proving that food is more than just sustenance—it is medicine for the mind.

Every recipe, every meal plan, and every nutritional insight shared here has been carefully designed to **support your mood, balance your energy, and strengthen your body from the inside out**. By embracing **gut-healthy, anti-inflammatory, and nutrient-dense** foods, you are not just managing symptoms—you are reclaiming your power, your clarity, and your peace.

Beyond the Plate: A Lifestyle of Wellness

This book is not just about food; it's about **building a sustainable lifestyle that supports your well-being**. True mental health is a combination of **nourishing meals, movement, mindfulness, and self-compassion**. As you move forward, keep these key principles in mind:

Consistency is key – Small, steady changes create long-lasting impact.

Pay attention to your body—it communicates its needs. Respect and respond to them.

Stay mindful of triggers – Avoid foods that fuel mood swings and instability.

Balance is everything – Mental wellness is about **harmony, not perfection**.

You are not alone – Healing happens in community. Seek support when needed.

Your Next Steps

You now have the tools, the recipes, and the knowledge to **take charge of your mental health through food**. Start where you are. Try new recipes, build your meal plans, and observe how your body and mind respond. Let food become your ally, your fuel, and your foundation for a **balanced and thriving life**.

Bipolar disorder may be a part of your story, but **it does not define you**. You have the power to nourish yourself, stabilize your mood, and cultivate a life filled with **vitality, clarity, and strength**.

To Your Health, Stability, and Joy—One Meal at a Time!

Made in the USA
Monee, IL
19 May 2025